RAILWAY MOODS

KEIGHLEY & WORTH VALLEY RAILWAY

MIKE HEATH

HALSGROVE

First published in Great Britain in 2005

British Library Cataloguing-in-Publication Data
A CIP record for this title is available from the British Library

ISBN 1 84114 442 8

HALSGROVE
Halsgrove House
Lower Moor Way
Tiverton, Devon EX16 6SS
Tel: 01884 243242
Fax: 01884 243325
email: sales@halsgrove.com
website: www.halsgrove.com

Printed and bound by D'Auria Industrie Grafiche Spa, Italy

For further information and advice about the Keighley and Worth Valley Railway,
contact Haworth Station, Keighley, West Yorkshire BD22 8NJ.
Telephone the 24 hour information line 01535 647777, or visit the website at www.kwvr.co.uk

INTRODUCTION

The Worth Valley stretches in a south-westerly direction from the Yorkshire town of Keighley, following the River Worth past the village of Oakworth and then its tributary, Bridgehouse Beck, through Haworth and Oxenhope to the moorland beyond.

In his book, *Moods of the Brontë Moors,* John Morrison referred to a great attraction of the area being the close proximity of town and country. Nowhere is this more evident than in the Worth Valley. The Keighley and Worth Valley Railway runs between Keighley and Oxenhope and though only 5 miles apart the contrast between these locations is striking. The former a typically busy town, with its boundaries being extended by the seemingly compulsory development of retail parks, the latter a quiet village set timelessly amongst wooded meadows surrounded by moorland.

Opened in 1865, the railway, which, like countless other branches, was built to connect local industry with the nearest main line, continued to transport passengers and goods for over ninety-five years until a combination of changing travel habits and antagonistic government policy, brought about its eventual closure in 1962.

There the story would have ended but for a small group of people determined to save the line. They established a Preservation Society, and set up an Operating Company to commence negotiations for the purchase of the line, and seek permission to operate it. These complex negotiations were long drawn out and it is thanks to the patience and perseverance of those initial Society members that on Saturday 29 June 1968 the Grand Reopening Train left Keighley for its historic run to Oxenhope. Thus were laid the foundations for what became an all year round service with steam-operated trains running every weekend.

The tasks that faced them cannot be understated. The Society took ownership of 5 miles of running track, five stations, thirty bridges, two tunnels, a number of culverts, and many other railway bits and pieces. As you can imagine, given the years of neglect prior to closure, these assets were not in the best of condition. Without the dedication of the hundreds of volunteers that have been involved in the restoration and maintenance of the Worth Valley branch line in its entirety, the memory and romance of a bygone age would have been lost for ever.

What follows is a personal photographic journey along the length of the line, and back, starting at Keighley, pausing to take a look at each of the stations, and the locomotive shed, as we travel towards the terminus at Oxenhope. The railway is viewed from all angles, across all four seasons, at all times of day, and night.

It was this line that launched my interest in railway photography. You may deduce that I have visited the railway many times!

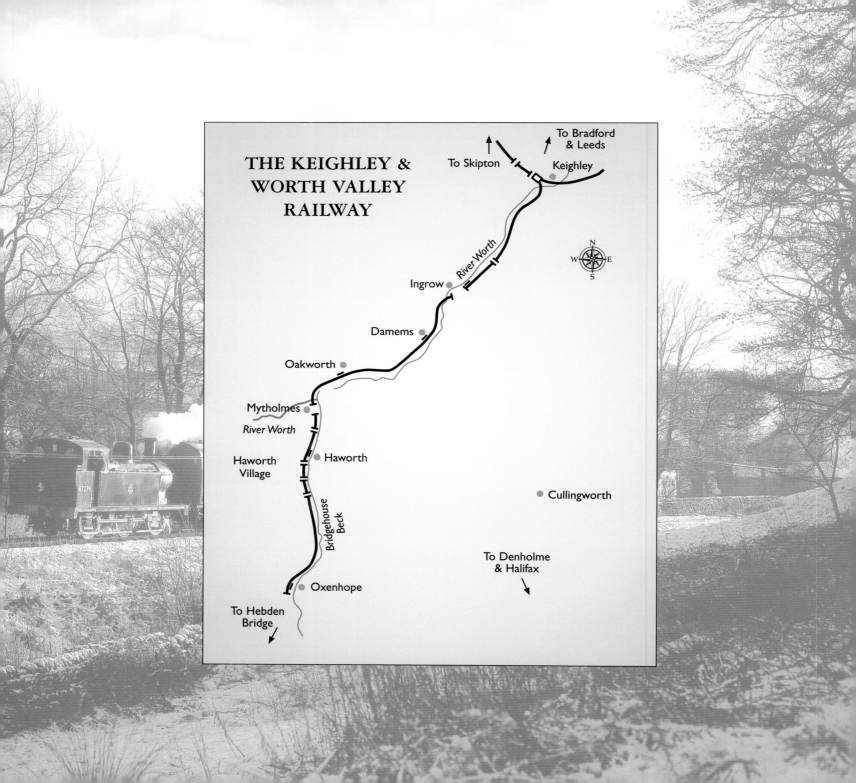

THE KEIGHLEY & WORTH VALLEY RAILWAY

To Skipton

To Bradford & Leeds

Keighley

River Worth

Ingrow

Damems

Oakworth

Mytholmes

River Worth

Haworth Village

Haworth

Cullingworth

Bridgehouse Beck

To Denholme & Halifax

Oxenhope

To Hebden Bridge

47279

Keighley, where the poster board which would once have proclaimed day returns to locations around Northern England, now gives the visitor information on the services provided by the volunteer-run Preservation Society.

The 'White Rose Pullman' offers the opportunity to dine with style in the luxurious surroundings of Pullman carriages. Diners relax in the glow of the table lamps in this nocturnal scene recreating the golden age of steam.

Opposite: Ornate cast iron columns support a glass canopy protecting travellers from the Yorkshire weather as they purchase their tickets for a journey back in time.

Over the years the railway has provided locations for many films and television programmes. On this occasion Keighley Station has taken on the guise of Bradford Exchange Station for a feature film. Cast and crew have a break between takes.

A reminder of the days when all freight and works trains were in the charge of the guard in his van at the rear of the train.

The intention of the Preservation Society has been to re-create the best aspects of a 1950's branch line. This night-time shot of platform 4 is evidence of their success.

Opposite: There's nothing more atmospheric than a working steam locomotive at night.

Passengers of all ages watch the engine back onto the carriages which will shortly transport them on a journey that will rekindle old memories for some and create new ones for others.

You can almost feel the cold with this winter scene. (However I have to confess that this is the one photograph in the book for which I cannot take credit. It was taken by my younger son, Karl, when he was only ten years old! My own camera equipment succumbed to the freezing temperatures on this occasion.)

On selected dates the railway runs vintage trains with carriages borrowed from the Vintage Carriage Museum at Ingrow. Here the 1888 built 'Coal Tank' locomotive prepares to depart.

Trains run between Christmas and New Year under the title 'Mince Pie Specials' with the last departure at dusk.

Ready for the off as the fire is coaled and boiler pressure forces steam through the safety valves.

And at twilight the glow of the fires lights up the footplates as the driver awaits the 'Right Away'.

A turntable demonstration is in full swing as the diesel railbus leaves with a shuttle service to Damems.

With a 1 in 58 gradient to tackle, the climb away from Keighley is rarely quiet, but imagine the sound that heralded this particular departure when competitors in a Town Crier competition visited the line.

A stormy departure under a thunderous sky.

The last light of a winter's day casts a golden glow as the locomotive makes a volcanic start to the journey.

As if the gradient wasn't challenging enough, trains leave Keighley by a sharp right hand curve, the severity of which can clearly be determined in this photograph.

The same location viewed from the adjacent cobbled street which is itself a reminder of days gone by.

Glorious weather conditions highlight the varnished teak finish of the former Metropolitan coaches in this vintage train formation.

Ye olde air conditioning in the form of opening windows affords passengers a clear view of the passing scenery and the occasional photographer.

Two locomotives combine to double-head a train on the climb beneath a row of terraced houses cut into the valley side.

The approach to the summit of Keighley bank is a favourite location for railway photographers with locomotives having to work hard, thus providing that much sought-after dramatic exhaust effect.

The 'going-away shot' is often much more atmospheric.

This temporarily-redundant buffer stop provided an unusual frame for this recreated typical branch line freight train scene.

With steam to spare, condensing in the cold winter air, the locomotive has passed over the summit and is getting into its stride as the gradient eases.

Opposite: Prior to Christmas, Santa visits the railway to distribute presents to all children booked on the December weekend specials. Here, at the top of the bank, the Santa Special heads towards a setting sun.

The first train of the day disturbs a landscape of new fallen snow as it emerges into the sunshine and scurries along the stretch of line known as the Great Northern Straight. This is so called because this section of the route was once shared with Keighley to Bradford and Halifax branches operated by the Great Northern Railway.

Opposite: For its Steam Gala Weekends, usually held twice a year in spring and autumn, the railway often hires in locomotives from other preservation societies. In May 2000 the Lakeside and Haverthwaite Railway in Cumbria provided their recently restored former Furness Railway Locomotive No.20 which was built originally in 1863!

After 1¼ miles the first station encountered is Ingrow West. (This designation is to distinguish it from Ingrow East which was located on the old Halifax line.) Framed by the arch beneath a road bridge, a freight train approaches the station.

The station building now seen at Ingrow, which opened in 1989, has an interesting history of its own. Due to vandalism the original building had to be demolished and the Society set about raising funds, through donations, for the purchase of a replacement. When sufficient funds had been secured the decision was made to buy the Midland station building from Foulridge on the former Skipton to Colne line. The building was dismantled, transported to Ingrow and rebuilt stone by stone. Yes, a Lancastrian building now sits on Yorkshire soil and blends well with the rest of line. The main benefactor was Geoffrey Reeday, who dedicated the foundation stone to the memory of his father who had frequently used the station.

Keeping with the freight theme this beautifully restored, former British Railways, Mechanical Horse and trailer was photographed by the station building. I doubt that its previous owners maintained it in this splendid condition.

Opposite: As night falls traditional Midland Railway oil lamps illuminate the scene as a short freight train pauses at the platform.

The station forecourt is often used by other societies to display their own preservation projects such as this impressive line-up of Austin cars.

The Vintage Carriage Trust Museum of Rail Travel is located at Ingrow and exhibits can often be seen operating in the yard. Captured here is former contractor's locomotive 'Sir Berkeley' built in 1891, for use on railway construction works, coupled to the oldest carriage in their collection, a four-wheeled tricomposite coach built in 1876. The term tricomposite referring to the three classes of accommodation provided, being one first, one second and two third class compartments.

With all train departure times clearly chalked on the station notice board our train prepares to leave.

On departing Ingrow the line dives into a short dark tunnel emerging between tall mill buildings. Passing on a shuttle service to Damems is the railway's heritage diesel multiple unit.

A wanderer returns, albeit temporarily. The locomotive pictured was resident at the Worth Valley in the early days of preservation, before relocating to the Great Central Railway in Loughborough. In 1998 it visited to take part in the railways thirtieth anniversary celebrations.

The road ahead from the trackside as the line again starts to climb steeply leaving the urban environment behind.

A field full of Lupins fills the foreground in this view of the train climbing on the approach to the next station, Damems.

Opposite: Here the surrounding countryside begins to take on a more rural aspect.

Damems is the smallest 'full-size' station in Britain, having a ticket-cum-station master's office, waiting room, toilet, signal box and station house.

The platform is only just long enough to accommodate one coach but is a particularly picturesque location from which to watch the trains pass by.

The station was built to serve a small mill close by, hence the narrowness of the cobbled lane that crosses the line, seen here as the train continues on its way up the valley.

Opposite: Not content with providing all necessary facilities this tiny station also controls a level crossing.

Just above Damems is a passing loop where on peak service days trains cross with those travelling in the opposite direction. With the Worth Valley line being a single track this is the only way of running more than one train at a time.

Opposite: A train from Keighley enters the loop drawing to a halt opposite the signal box. When a two train service is operating, the signal box will be open and tokens are exchanged between the signalman and the train crew. A token, which is in fact a key token, is a brass casting that carries the name of the single line section. These tokens are electronically released from a token instrument, giving authority for the train to be on that single line section, thereby safeguarding against head-on collisions. The signalman will use the key to unlock the levers controlling the points, giving the train from Oxenhope access to the run-round loop.

The train travelling down to Keighley then enters the loop, slowly drifting past the signal box, allowing its crew to hand the token for the Oxenhope section of line to the signalman whilst, at the same time, receiving that for the Keighley section.

With the Keighley-bound train disappearing in the distance, the signalman has handed the Oxenhope section token to the crew of locomotive 5305, triggered the signal and, with his work complete for now, pauses to watch it leave.

On a cold October morning the departure from the loop is viewed from the A629 Halifax road high up the valley side.

Opposite: A few moments later the locomotive exhaust hangs in the still air as the train, now in open country, climbs towards Oakworth.

Several months later and the trees have shed their leaves giving a clear view of Oakworth Station (centre left) and the village of that name, located on the hillside half a mile above it.

In perfect weather conditions this side-on view captures the train rounding the hillside at the start of the ascent.

Oakworth Bank is another location favoured by many railway photographers as the locomotives again have to work hard, creating that dramatic exhaust effect, or 'clag' as it is known. From time to time I have joined the gallery that assembles here, capturing scenes such as this colourful combination.

Standing on the platform the sound of an approaching train can be heard long before it comes into view.

Maintained in its Edwardian splendour, Oakworth Station is kept as near as possible in its 1905-1914 condition.

Opposite: Listen carefully and you just might hear Station Porter Perks's cry of '*Oakworth*' as the train pulls into the station. This was of course the main location of the EMI production of E. Nesbit's *The Railway Children* filmed during 1969/1970.

Occasionally amateur dramatic societies attend the line to perform cameo scenes from the classics. Here Sherlock Holmes and Dr Watson no doubt recall their many adventures that have involved railways, most of which have been filmed on the KWVR at one time or another.

Gas lamps, platform trolleys, milk churns, luggage, Edwardian posters and neat gardens all help to retain the old world atmosphere.

The station interior is also lit by gas, giving a golden glow to the station master's desk which does not appear to have changed since the first arrival was recorded over a century ago.

Every five years the re-opening of the line, 29 June 1968, is celebrated by decorating the locomotive in service, over the appropriate weekend, as for that special occasion. The 35th anniversary was notable for the fact that former British Railways Class 2MT 2-6-2 side tank engine No. 41241 was working, just as it was on that inaugural day.

Small goods yards and sidings were commonplace alongside village stations and Oakworth was no exception. Nowadays it is used by the railway's permanent way department for storage.

It is time to get back on the train as the footplate crew await a wave of the guard's green flag.

On leaving Oakworth the railway enters a small wooded area. Taken in the shade of the trees, this photograph captures the glint on a pair of locomotives working hard as they head on up the valley.

Opposite: To most travellers a ride behind a steam locomotive is exciting enough. Enthusiasts, however, look for a little extra and are well catered for on Gala Weekends. In 1997 former Midland Railway class 1F side tank locomotive 41708, which was built in 1880, visited the line recreating images from the 1920s when some Worth Valley services were in the hands of these engines.

The magic combination of snow, sun and steam is not always easy to find in Britain. Here all three are in great abundance on the approach to Mytholmes viaduct.

Opposite: Picture the scene; you want to photograph an authentic vintage Metropolitan Railway train on the climb towards Haworth. In glorious sunshine you set up your camera and frame the scene within the surrounding tree branches hoping that the engine will have a pure white exhaust to set against the clear blue sky. The train can be heard approaching, you pray that the sun stays out and no vehicles cross the bridge as it passes. It rarely goes that well!

The footplate crew have to work hard to maintain the steam pressure necessary to drive the train on up the valley. The severity of the climb is evident in this low shot from the line side.

Low lighting adds to this moody impression of steam as American-built locomotive 5820, nicknamed *Big Jim*, and a favourite of my elder son Darren, crosses Mytholmes Viaduct.

It is at this point that the railway parts company with the River Worth to follow Bridgehouse Beck for the remainder of its course. The setting sun creates a warm autumnal glow over the landscape surrounding the approach to Mytholmes Tunnel.

The village of Oakworth is the backdrop to this scene taken from above the tunnel mouth.

Cold February air will ensure that the condensed exhaust will continue to roll out of the tunnel long after the train has gone.

Opposite: From the tunnel the line curves round the hillside on the approach to Haworth Station. The footpath running alongside at this point is part of The *Railway Children Walk* which is a way-marked route devised to enable the walker to visit the various locations used in the film.

Shortly before arriving at Haworth the site where the film finished is passed. It was here that all the cast were seen waving as Roberta (Jenny Agutter) writes *The End* on a chalkboard.

Three miles from the start of the journey in the manufacturing town of Keighley, the urban scene has given way to a landscape of villages and mills.

A Yorkshire 'Host of golden daffodils' welcomes springtime visitors to Haworth.

Opposite: Haworth, the village on the hill, looks down on the railway to see the next arrival at its station in the valley below.

Winter visitors huddle together in an effort to keep warm as they await their train.

The sun doesn't always shine on the railway!

Haworth Station is regarded as the headquarters of the line and in the adjacent yard stands the former Midland Railway warehouse, built for the wool traffic of the time, which is now used for the maintenance of the railway's locomotives.

Opposite: At night a warm glow covers the yard as the locomotives await the next day's duties.

Early risers can watch the steam locomotives being prepared for the day's work. Many volunteer hands work hard to ensure the engines are ready for the viewing public.

Opposite: The cleaners' work is done and the locomotives sparkle in the morning sun. Now attention is turned to tending the fire and oiling round the various parts of the motion.

Overhaul and restoration requires the dismantling of locomotives necessitating the use of some heavy lifting gear. In order to be able to carry out these works themselves a former British Railways breakdown crane was purchased by the Society.

The view from a footplate as a boiler is lifted clear of its frames.

In the evening when the locomotives have returned to the yard the footplate crew still have work to do. The dirty, arduous tasks of cleaning out the char from the smokeboxes, raking the ashpan and sometimes 'paddling out' the remains of the fire have to be carried out. Capturing the fire being thrown out with a time exposure photograph can produce spectacular results.

The locomotives have been put to bed for the night, the crews have retired for a shower, some supper, and perhaps a beverage or two. An eerie calm descends on the yard.

A vintage bus service provides a link with the village and the various Brontë tourist attractions, in high season.

The more energetic passenger will of course climb the cobbled road up to the Main Street having first traversed the railway's footbridge possibly pausing for a whiff of nostalgia as the train departs. However, please be aware that it can be difficult to wash a nostalgic whiff from your whites.

The view from the footbridge as the train passes alongside the locomotive shed heading towards the line's terminus at Oxenhope.

94

In the height of summer the journey continues past the loop connecting the main line to the shed yard.

Passing the same location in spring 1994 the locomotive carries a wreath attached to the smokebox in memory of the Preservation Society's first Chairman, and local Member of Parliament, Bob Cryer who had recently passed away.

It's an October Enthusiasts Weekend and the early morning locomotive movements can be seen from all round the valley.

Leaving the village on the hill behind, a vintage train scurries along through the countryside in the morning sun.

Opposite: A covering of snow and the scene becomes a winter wonderland.

Double-heading of trains during special events can create atmospheric scenes with this pairing being no exception as they power their way up the valley.

Opposite: Size isn't everything as this little and large combination proves, making light work of their own task as they pass on the rails.

Summer is here with a vintage train ambling past this lush scene with a carpet of buttercups and summer grasses filling the foreground to complete the picture.

Opposite: The *top field* is the title photographers have given to this particularly attractive location which is midway between Haworth and Oxenhope, and also crossed by *The Railway Children Walk* referred to earlier.

At this point the valley, still steep and severe, curves much more gently giving the line an almost straight path as it enters a tree-lined section.

A walker, following another of the many footpaths that criss-cross the area pauses to watch the train pass by.

You can almost hear the hiss of the crisp white steam escaping from the carriage heating pipes as, bathed in low winter sun, the train takes the curve on the last leg of the journey to Oxenhope.

Opposite: Trees can often form a natural frame for a photograph as here, where a vintage locomotive hauling historic coaches is captured in the Brontë countryside. A sprinkling of bluebells adds colour to this idyllic scene.

The same view in spring when the trees are green, the grass is growing and the heating has been turned off.

Opposite: Between Christmas and New Year passengers are treated to a glass of sherry and a mince pie as they travel along the line. A dusting of snow covers the valley as the Mince Pie Special approaches the terminus.

The morning sun picks out the train weaving its way through a winter landscape.

Opposite: Big Jim is not the only American-built locomotive to operate on this railway. No. 30072 was built in Pennsylvania in 1943 and was one of fifteen bought by the Southern Railway in 1946 for use as shunters at Southampton Docks.

Oxenhope, the line's terminus where passengers disembark to enjoy refreshments in the buffet car or visit the adjacent museum to view locomotives that are currently out of traffic.

Locomotives also require refreshment for the return journey but there's no automatic shut off to warn of a full tank.

After dark the station takes on an even more magical atmosphere.

Opposite: At Christmas festive illuminations and decorations welcome excited children visiting Santa, telling him of their requirements, relieving him of a present, and then forcing their dad to accompany them on a visit to the footplate.

Externally the station platform has creosoted fences, enamel advertisements and gas lighting as reminders of the past.

Internally the booking hall retains the welcoming atmosphere that has greeted passengers for many decades.

In October 1996, on the Saturday evening of the Enthusiast Weekend, Society members had the opportunity to photograph a demonstration freight train at night. The combination of photographing steam locomotives at night and travelling up the valley on the open back of the guard's van under the light of an autumn moon was a wonderful experience.

Rekindling memories of summer Sundays of bygone days when afternoons would often be accompanied by the sound of a brass band, the Hade Edge Band entertain passengers about to depart on the return journey to Keighley.

It is unusual for locomotives to face north towards Keighley making views such as this departure from Oxenhope quite rare.

Opposite: There's only the light from the platform gas lamps to accompany this night-time departure.

Leaving Oxenhope nestling in the foothills of the Pennines, the train passes through the autumn-tinted wooded section of the valley. The exhaust, hanging in the cold morning air, follows the curvature of the route so far.

Opposite: The more traditional tender first departure. Another Mince Pie Special in an ideal Christmas landscape.

Another winter scene taken from one of the many farm tracks cut into the side of the valley.

Opposite: The low winter sun highlights the whole length of the train as it emerges from the woods heading back to Haworth.

Passing top field on the return trip.

Here, top field forms the back drop as a demonstration freight passes. Bridgehouse Beck provides the foreground.

Cloaked against the cold this horse shows little interest in the approaching ensemble. Unlike a previous occasion when on hearing a distant whistle it raced forward to a position where it filled the frame of my viewfinder. Despite my vociferous requests for it to vacate the scene, it remained statuesque until the train had passed!

On normal service days the early morning trains are usually handled by the railway's heritage diesel fleet.

A few months later another departure is photographed a little further down the line.

Opposite: Only my and my son's footprints have disturbed the snow on the platform at Haworth as we made our way to a position from where we could capture this atmospheric winter scene.

Once a year the railway holds a weekend event for the ever-increasing number of enthusiasts who for some unknown reason prefer diesel-powered traction to steam.

Leaving Haworth and its daffodils behind, the train continues its descent alongside a swollen Bridgehouse Beck.

The same location where the early morning sun picks out the frost clinging to the autumn foliage.

Opposite: Oakworth; where else could you wait for a train in such peaceful surroundings?

Departure time again, as the footplate crew await permission to proceed.

Opposite: A last look at this country station as the rail bus heads off down the valley.

The descent of Oakworth Bank is made with steam to spare.

Tokens have been exchanged with the Oxenhope-bound train in the loop, and Damems Station is passed without stopping.

Passengers have boarded the vintage coaches at Ingrow for the return trip.

Opposite: Our destination, Keighley, comes into view in the distance.

The train rounds the curve at the bottom of the bank on the final approach to the station.

This is Keighley. The train and our journey terminates here. I hope that you have enjoyed the trip and that you will visit again, perhaps in person to take in the Keighley and Worth Valley Railway experience for yourself.

Now all that remains is to oil all round and get ready for the next trip.